20 WAYS TO COOK
POTATOES

David Grant has held positions as head chef and as catering manager, and has had regional responsibility for training young chefs. Now settled in an hotel, his high quality cuisine has gained him much credit and an out-standing reputation amongst regulars.

20 Ways to Cook
POTATOES

David J Grant

Thomas Harmsworth Publishing Company

First published 1994 by
Thomas Harmsworth Publishing
Company
Old Rectory Offices
Stoke Abbott
Beaminster
Dorset DT8 3JT
United Kingdom

British Library Cataloguing-in-Publication
Data. A catalogue record for this book is
available from the British Library.

ISSN 1355-4050
ISBN 0 948807 26 1

Printed and bound in Great Britain by
BPC Paulton Books Ltd

CONTENTS

INTRODUCTION

POTATO VARIETIES

There are many varieties of potato on the market today. Each has a unique texture. Buying the right potato is essential to ensure the best results when cooking. In the majority of cookery books it is difficult to find the information required. Seldom do they state the type of potato needed.

Below are listed the main varieties and the cookery processes to which they are best suited. Also listed are their seasons to help you when purchasing.

Boiling. Home Guard, Pentland Javelin, Ulster Sceptre, Alcmaria, Arran Comet, Première, Maris Bard, Wilja, Estima, Désirée, Maris Piper, Cara, Romano.

Creaming, puréeing and mashing. King Edward, Pentland Squire, Désirée.

Baking. Floury varieties such as: King Edward, Maris Piper, Pentland Squire, Cara, Estima, Romano, Wilja, Pentland Dell, Désirée.

Roasting and frying. For roasting and frying you need a potato that will retain a firmer texture. The best types for this are Désirée, Maris Piper, Pentland Crown, Romano (not for chips).

Seasonal information

June — July: Home Guard, Arran Comet, Ulster Sceptre, Maris Bard, Pentland Javelin, Alcmaria and Première.

August — March: Wilja and Estima.

September — May: Désirée, Maris Piper, Cara and Romano, King Edward.

BUYING TIPS

Look initially for a firm potato with good shape. Avoid those that are obviously blemished, scuffed or with any indication of germination (the presence of new shoots). More importantly do not buy those that have begun going green. They should be thrown away. Remember that the skin is an important source of nutrient, so avoid those with bruising or eyes. The variety of potato chosen depends on the recipe you are preparing. There are many different types of potato, each with a unique texture. But in general, a firm, waxy potato (usually new) is ideal for frying, etc. A floury potato (usually old crop) being best in purées and soups, and for mashing. When purchasing allow around 6 - 8 oz (175 - 225 gm) per portion. If you are able to select your own potatoes from a shop display always choose potatoes of a similar size to each other.

STORAGE OF POTATOES

Potatoes bruise easily. Ideally, buy in regularly, to avoid any being stored for too long. Sacks,

paper bags or vegetable racks are best for storage. If purchased in plastic bags, remove the potatoes, as the bags cause them to sweat. This will turn them mouldy or cause them to go off quickly. Store in a cool, dry and dark place, avoiding light, as it spoils the potato and turns them green.

Try not to prepare potatoes too far in advance. They should be kept in cold water once peeled, although if kept in such conditions for periods of three hours or longer the outsides will harden, prolonging the cooking time.

PREPARATION TECHNIQUES

Preparing potatoes. Peel with care, removing any eyes with a vegetable corer or small knife. Place potatoes immediately in cold water to prevent discolouring. Check your recipe before peeling, as some require the potatoes to be rinsed, whereas others require them unrinsed to retain starch.

Only prepare potatoes as and when required. As with other vegetables, the nutrients lie close to the skin and can easily be lost.

For personal safety always use a sharp knife when preparing any vegetable.

Cuts of potato. There are many cuts and shapes for potatoes. Listed below are just a few of the more commonly used ones.

Barrel-shaped — It helps, and saves wastage, if evenly sized potatoes are used. Trim off the top and the bottom of the potato, giving you two flat surfaces. If using a large potato, cut in half. Holding the potato by the ends you have just cut, work your way around the potato from bot-

tom to top cutting and retaining an oval shape. You should ideally end up with a potato that has 6 - 8 sides of even width. Try not to remove too much of the potato.

Parisienne — These are ball shapes which are made using a special scoop, similar to a small ice-cream scoop. If purchasing, ask for a parisienne scoop.

Small dice — Cut the potato into convenient sized lengths. Cut the lengths into ½ inch (1.25 cm) slices. Cut the slices into ½ inch (1.25 cm) strips. Then the strips into ½ inch (1.25 cm) cubes.

Any trimmings left over from the cuts listed can be used for puréed, mashed or creamed potatoes, but check the type of potato and its suitability for the recipe.

EQUIPMENT REQUIRED

The following equipment is required in the recipes in this book:

    Large and small cook's knife
    Measuring jug
    Chopping board
    Electric liquidizer or blender
    Sieve
    Cheese grater
    Soufflé dish
    Fish slice
    Colander
    Small measuring/weighing scales
    Corer
    Peeler
    Steel or plastic bowls
    Pastry brush
    Piping bag and star nozzle

Potato masher
Plastic spatula
Shallow frying pan
Deep frying pan
Selection of saucepans
Tablespoon, teaspoon and fork
Garlic press
Casserole dish
Rolling pin
Turning knife
Slotted spoon
Tin-opener
Whisk
Loaf tins
Baking tray
Parisienne scoop
Wooden spoons

COOKING PROCESSES

Boiling. Cut the cleaned (and peeled, if wished) potatoes into even-sized pieces, cover with cold water and 1 - 2 teaspoons of salt per 1 lb (450 gm) of potatoes. Bring to the boil, reduce heat and simmer for 10 - 15 minutes, depending on the size and cut of the potato used. If not being used immediately, place under cold running water to prevent further cooking. Once cool, drain.

New potatoes should be placed in already-boiling, salted water. If the potatoes are of an uneven size, place the large ones in first and phase the remainder into the boiling water at approximately 30 second intervals, down to the smallest. This will ensure that they are all ready at about the same time.

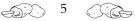

The addition of two or three sprigs of fresh mint much enhances the flavour. Remove the mint before draining the potatoes to avoid its clinging to either the colander or the potatoes themselves. As an alternative, or as well, a sprinkling of fresh, chopped parsley or chives on the buttered potatoes also enhances the flavour and appearance.

Mashing. Boil old potatoes, drain and dry off in a saucepan over a very gentle heat. Mash with a potato masher or fork.

Creaming. Cook as for mashed potato, then add 1 oz (25 gm) butter and 3 - 4 tablespoons of milk, beating in well. Use these measurements for every 1 lb (450 gm) of potatoes. Season well and continue beating until smooth and creamy. Turn out into a serving dish, marking the top with a fork. Sprinkle with chopped parsley.

Puréeing. Used for piping, this potato has to be extremely smooth. You can either rub the potatoes (boiled) through a sieve. Or, using a food processor, purée until smooth. Once puréed, beat in 2 oz (50 gm) butter along with 1 egg yolk, or a whole egg and a touch of cream. These measurements apply to 1 lb (450 gm) of potatoes.

Baking. Choose even-sized potatoes. Scrub well and remove any eyes. Prick randomly with a fork. Place in an oven warmed to 400F/200C/gas mark 6. Cook until soft to pinch (around ¾ - 1¼ hours, depending on the size of potato). To serve, cut a cross in the top and squeeze gently at the base to open slightly. Then add a little butter and, if desired, some grated cheese.

Roasting. Old potatoes are best used for roasting. Peel and cut into even-sized pieces. Place into a saucepan of cold water with a little salt. Bring to the boil and simmer for 4 - 5 minutes. Drain well. Heat a roasting tray containing 4 oz (125 gm) lard or dripping, add the potatoes carefully and baste well. Place in hot oven 400F/200C/gas mark 6 for about 25 minutes or until browning has begun. Then turn and baste again, returning to the oven for a further 25 minutes or until well brown and tender within. You may roast your potatoes without par-boiling, in which case allow around 10 - 15 minutes longer. To obtain more flavour roast the potatoes around the joint of meat.

Sautéing. Boil until barely tender, then drain well. Cut into slices about ¼ inch (0.5 cm) thick or dice into ¼ inch (0.5 cm) cubes. Melt ¼ - ½ oz (5 - 10 gm) of butter, lard or oil into a frying pan and fry potatoes until golden brown all over. Drain well and serve, lightly seasoned, and with chopped parsley.

Frying (chips). Peel potatoes and cut into desired size around ¼ - ½ inch (0.5 - 1.25 cm) thick, then into strips, evenly sized. Soak for 30 minutes to remove any excess starch. Drain well and dry thoroughly. Heat a pan of oil, no more than half full, to 375F/190C. Place chips into a wire basket and lower gently, cooking for 7 - 8 minutes. Remember not to over-fill the basket. Once lightly coloured and cooked remove and dry on kitchen paper. Before serving chips, return to the fat and fry for a further 4 minutes, or until crisp and golden brown. To serve, lightly season with salt and pepper. An addition of grated cheese, lightly browned under a grill is also tasty.

Game chips are cooked in the same way as above, allowing less time for the initial frying. In this instance the potatoes should be cut into very thin slices before frying.

Microwaving. For a quick and easy way to produce a meal for one, take a medium-sized potato 8 oz (225 gm), scrub it clean and pat it dry. Ensuring that all cuts are lengthways, take a sharp knife and cut the potato in half. Cut each piece in half again and each of the resulting quarters in half so that you have 8 pieces. Place these in one layer in a microwavable dish, add 1 tablespoon of water and cover with microwavable film. Pierce the film to let steam escape and place in the microwave oven. Your potato will cook in six minutes at full power in a 650w oven. Take the hot potato and cover with a topping of your choice. For instance, sprinkle with some grated cheese and put back in the oven for 1 minute on full power.

There are any number of potential toppings you can place on the cooked potato.

DRESSINGS, SAUCES AND STOCKS

VINAIGRETTE
3 - 6 tablespoons olive oil
1 teaspoon french mustard
1 tablespoon vinegar (tarragon, white wine etc)
salt and pepper

Combine all ingredients and mix well.

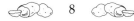

WHITE STOCK

2¼ lbs (1 kg) raw chicken bones
3¾ pints (2 litres) water
1 lb (450 gm) vegetables (onion, carrot, celery and leek)
bouquet garni (thyme, bayleaf and parsley stalks)
12 peppercorns

Chop the bones and remove any fat. Place into a saucepan, add water and bring to the boil.

Skim and wipe round the sides of the pan, simmer gently. Add vegetables and bouquet garni with peppercorns. Simmer for 6 - 8 hours, skim and strain.

Your butcher will often be happy to give you bones.

BROWN STOCK

Use the same ingredients as for the white stock with the addition of a few mushroom trimmings and tomatoes.

Chop the bones and brown well on all sides in a frying pan with some oil (see page 11).

Place the bones in a roasting tin and put it in a preheated oven (425F/220C/gas mark 7), and cook for 30 - 45 minutes. Drain off any fat and remove the bones to a saucepan.

Brown the sediment left in the roasting tin, and add 1 pint (550 ml) of water. Boil and simmer for a few minutes, then add to the bones in the saucepan. Bring to the boil again and skim with a ladle.

Wash, peel and roughly chop the vegetables. Fry them in a little oil until well browned, then add to the bones. Add the bouquet garni and peppercorns. Simmer for 6 - 8 hours. Skim and strain.

Chef's tip:
☆ When making either the white or the brown stock, put in a handful of ice cubes just before they start boiling for the first time. This brings all the scum to the top and aids skimming.

MORNAY SAUCE

4 oz (125 gm) butter
4 oz (125 gm) flour
1¾pints (1 litre) milk
½ onion studded with cloves
4 oz (125 gm) grated Cheddar cheese
2 egg yolks

Warm the milk gently until just off the boil, then remove from the heat and place to one side.

Melt the butter in a thick-bottomed pan.

Add the flour and mix in (this is called a *roux*). Cook for about two minutes over a very gentle heat and cool.

Gradually add the warmed milk and stir until smooth. Add the studded onion. Simmer for 30 minutes, stirring often.

Remove the onion, add the grated cheese and the egg yolks, and mix well.

Cook for a further 5 minutes until the cheese has melted. Pass through a strainer or liquidize in a food processor.

Peeling tomatoes (the scalding method)
Cut a small cross in the base of the tomato to be

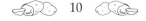

peeled. Plunge into boiling water for between 10 - 20 seconds depending on the ripeness of the tomato. Drain immediately and cover with cold water and allow to cool, remove the skin, cut in half and take out the seeds.

Roughly chop the flesh, unless otherwise stated in recipe.

COOKING TERMS AND DEFINITIONS

The following list of cooking terms may be encountered within this book, or generally, in vegetable cookery. Reference to the list will improve understanding and simplify the use of these recipes.

Assaisonner — to season

Au four — baked in the oven

Au beurre — with butter

Basting — spooning melted fat over the food during cooking

Blanching — placing a food for a very short time into boiling water

Bouquet garni — a mixture of parsley stalks, thyme and bayleaf

Brown — the colouring of food with the application of heat

Brunoise — small dice

Casserole — an earthenware fireproof dish with a lid

Chauffant — a pan of hot salted water used for re-heating vegetables

Concasser — refers to tomatoes. To place in boiling water for ten seconds, then cooling in cold water (refreshing), removing the skin and seeds, and roughly chopping

Croquettes — Refers mainly to potatoes moulded into cylinder shapes and deep-fried in egg and breadcrumbs

Drain — to place food into a colander

Garnish — the trimmings upon a dish

Hors d'œuvre — appetising first course

Jardinière — vegetables cut into batons

Julienne — cut into fine strips

Mirepoix — roughly cut carrots, onion, celery, with a sprig of thyme and a bayleaf

Paysanne — cut into shapes, thin pieces

Refresh — to cool under cold running water, so as to prevent from cooking further

Season — to add salt and pepper

Skimming — removing surface scum etc using a ladle.

Soufflé — a very light dish, hot or cold

Strain — to separate the liquid from the solid

Sweat — to cook in fat under a lid without colour

Tossing — the turning of food to ensure a thorough coat

TABLE OF OVEN TEMPERATURES

	Fahrenheit (F)	Celsius (C)	Gas mark
	150	70	
	175	80	
	200	100	
Very cool	225	110	¼
	250	120	½
	275	140	1
Cool	300	150	2
Warm	325	160	3

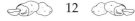

Moderate/			
Medium	350	180	4
Fairly Hot	375	190	5
	400	200	6
Hot	425	220	7
	450	230	8
Very hot	475	240	9
	500	260	9

IMPERIAL/METRIC CONVERSIONS

Dry weight		**Liquid measure**	
ounces	grams	fluid ounces	millilitres
1	25	1	25
2	50	2	50
3	75	3	75-90
4 (¼ lb)	125	4	125
5	150	5 (¼ pint)	150
6	175	6	175
7	200	7	200
8 (½ lb)	225	8	225
9	250	9	250
10	275	10 (½ pint)	275
11	300	11	300
12 (¾ lb)	350	12	350
13	375	13	375
14	400	14	400
15	425	15 (¾ pint)	425
16 (1 lb)	450	16	450
17	475	17	475
18	500	18	500
2¼ lb	1000 (1 kilo)	20 (1 pint)	550
		1¾ pints	1000 (1 litre)

DUCHESSE POTATOES AND DERIVATIVES

Serves: 3 per lb (450 gm) of potatoes
Type of dish: hot vegetable or garnish
Preparation time: basic recipe 30 - 35 minutes
Waiting time: 15 minutes
Cooking time: 2 - 3 minutes
Suitable for dinner parties: yes
Suitable for first course: yes, as garnish to fish
Suitable for microwave cooking: yes, with grill
Suitable for pressure cooking: no
Special equipment: potato masher and piping
  bag with star nozzle
Suitable for freezing: no
Calorie content: low
Carbohydrate content: low
Fibre content: low
Protein content: low
Fat content: low

2 lb (1 kg) potatoes ·	
2 egg yolks	
2 oz (50 gm) butter	
salt and pepper	

Wash, peel and rewash the potatoes and cut into small dice. Cook in salted water. Drain off the water, cover with a lid and return to a low heat to dry out the potatoes.

Pass through a sieve or mash well. Place the potatoes in a clean bowl. Add the egg yolks and stir in vigorously with a wooden spoon. Mix in the butter and correct the seasoning.

Place in a piping bag fitted with a large star tube. Pipe out in neat spirals around 1 inch (2.5 cm) diameter and 2 inches (5 cm) high onto a lightly-greased baking sheet.

Place into a hot oven for 2 - 3 minutes to slightly harden the outside. Remove from the oven, brush the edges with beaten egg and brown under the grill.

DERIVATIVES

Galette potatoes — Duchesse mixture moulded into flat cakes 1½ inch (3.75 cm) diameter, ½ inch (1.25 cm) thick. Shallow fry on both sides in very hot oil, and serve.

Brioche potatoes — Duchesse mixture shaped into the shape of a cottage loaf, i.e. 1 inch (2.5 cm) diameter ball with a ½ inch (1.25 cm) diameter ball on top pierced completely through

with a small knife. Place in a hot oven to harden the surface. Brush with beaten egg and brown under the grill.

Croquette potatoes — Duchesse mixture moulded into cylinder shapes 2 by 1 inches (5 by 2.5 cm). Roll them in flour, egg wash and breadcrumbs. Reshape with a palette knife and deep fry in hot oil until golden brown. Drain and serve.

Almond potatoes — Prepare and cook as for croquette potatoes replacing the breadcrumbs with nibbed almonds.

Marquis potatoes — Pipe duchesse mixture in the shape of a nest around 2 by 1 inches (5 by 2.5 cm). Bake in a hot oven until the outside has hardened. Brush with beaten egg and brown under the grill. Serve filled with chopped tomato and parsley.

Chef's tip:
☆ When mashing the potatoes for the original duchesse recipe make sure that the potato has no lumps, as this will cause the piping bag to block.

DEVILLED POTATO SALAD WITH FRANKFURTERS

Serves: 4

Type of dish: cold lunch or starter

Preparation time: 20 - 25 minutes including cooking potatoes

Waiting time: 30 minutes for cooling

Cooking time: potatoes only

Suitable for dinner parties: yes

Suitable for first course: yes

Suitable for microwave cooking: no

Suitable for pressure cooking: no

Special equipment: none

Suitable for freezing: no

Calorie content: average

Carbohydrate content: average

Fibre content: low

Protein content: average

Fat content: low

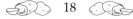

I lb (450 gm) potatoes
3 fl oz (75 ml) French dressing
I garlic clove crushed
2 teaspoons french mustard
¼ teaspoon Worcestershire sauce
pinch of cayenne pepper
3 tomatoes skinned and chopped
I green pepper
6 spring onions
salt and ground black pepper
I teaspoon paprika
8 - 10 cooked frankfurters

Peel and dice the potatoes into ¼ inch (½ cm) dice.

Cook the potatoes in boiling salted water for 10 - 15 minutes until tender and cooked.

Drain the potatoes well.

Mix the dressing, garlic, mustard, Worcestershire sauce and cayenne pepper together. Then add the potatoes stirring well. Cool completely. Skin and chop the tomatoes, core, seed and dice the pepper and chop the spring onions. When the potatoes are cold add the tomatoes, peppers, spring onions, and salt and pepper to taste.

Serve in a salad dish. Sprinkle with paprika and arrange the frankfurters around the edge.

Chef's tip:
☆ As an alternative to frankfurters, cold sliced chicken or garlic sausage may be used. Also,

this particular dish is ideal for using up any
cooked meat left over from Sunday lunch.

POTATO AND APPLE CAKE

Serves: 4
Type of dish: hot pudding
Preparation time: 25 - 30 minutes
Waiting time: 15 - 20 minutes
Cooking time: 30 minutes
Suitable for dinner parties: no
Suitable for first course: no
Suitable for microwave cooking: no
Suitable for pressure cooking: no
Special equipment: potato masher and rolling
   pin
Suitable for freezing: no
Calorie content: low
Carbohydrate content: average
Fibre content: low
Protein content: average
Fat content: low

 21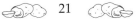

1 lb (450 gm) potatoes	
3 oz (75 gm) butter	
1 tablespoon (15 ml) milk	
4 oz (125 gm) flour	
¼ teaspoon baking powder	
½ teaspoon of salt	
4 teaspoons sugar	
½ teaspoon of cinnamon or mixed spice	
2 small eating apples, peeled and cored	
cream to serve	

Peel, roughly-dice and cook the potatoes in boiling salted water until tender and cooked.

Drain and mash using a potato masher or fork.

Peel and core the apples.

Melt 1 oz (25 gm) of the butter and add it to the potatoes with the milk. Add the flour, baking powder and salt, and work in.

Place onto a floured top, roll out to a thickness of about ¾ inch (2 cm) and cut into 4 even-sized pieces.

On two of these pile slices of raw apple. Place the other two pieces on top. Then press the edges together. Bake in a preheated 350F / 180C / gas mark 4 oven until brown (about 20 minutes).

When cooked, slit each cake around the sides and remove the tops laying them brown-side down. Divide the apples between the tops and bottoms. Dot with the remaining butter and sprinkle them with the sugar and cinnamon.

Return to the oven until the butter has melted, about four minutes.

Serve at once with cream.

☆　　☆　　☆

Chef's tip:
☆ Do not prepare the apples too far in advance
as they will brown quickly.

VICHYSSOISE SOUP

Serves: 6
Type of dish: cold starter
Preparation time: 30 minutes
Waiting time: 1 - 2 hours to chill
Cooking time: 30 minutes
Suitable for dinner parties: yes
Suitable for first course: yes
Suitable for microwave cooking: yes
Suitable for pressure cooking: no
Special equipment: electric liquidizer or
    blender
Suitable for freezing: yes
Calorie content: average
Carbohydrate content: average
Fibre content: low
Protein content: average
Fat content: average

3 leeks
1½ oz (35 gm) butter
1 onion, peeled and sliced thinly
1 lb (450 gm) potatoes, peeled and diced
1½ pints (825 ml) white stock
salt and pepper
½ teaspoon ground coriander
1 egg yolk
¼ pint (150 ml) single cream
chopped herbs (chives, parsley and coriander)

Remove the green part of the leeks and slice remainder thinly. Peel and dice the potatoes. Peel and thinly slice the onions.

Melt the butter in a saucepan, then add the leeks and onions.

Fry for 5 minutes gently, stirring frequently, without browning.

Add potatoes, stock, salt, pepper and coriander and bring to the boil.

Cover and simmer for 30 minutes until vegetables are tender.

Purée in an electric liquidizer and place in a clean pan.

Blend the egg yolk with the cream.

Add a little of the soup and whisk back into the rest of the soup in the saucepan.

Reheat gently but do not reboil, or it will separate.

Cool and chill thoroughly.

Serve in bowls, sprinkled with chopped chives, parsley and coriander.

☆　　☆　　☆

Chef's tips:

☆ To make leek and potato soup, leave the green parts on the leeks and cook as recipe. Serve hot.

☆ If you have not got an electric liquidizer, use a sieve or conical strainer.

☆ Coriander may be omitted from the recipe. It is optional.

SHEPHERD'S PIE

Serves: 6
Type of dish: hot main course
Preparation time: 50 minutes - 1 hour
Waiting time: 1 hour 25 minutes
Cooking time: 2 hours 15 minutes
Suitable for dinner parties: no
Suitable for first course: no
Suitable for microwave cooking: no
Suitable for pressure cooking: no
Special equipment: casserole dish
Suitable for freezing: base only
Calorie content: average
Carbohydrate content: high
Fibre content: low
Protein content: high
Fat content: average

1½ lb (675 gm) minced lamb
4 tablespoons olive oil
1 large onion
2 garlic cloves
4 large tomatoes
2 carrots
¾ pint (425 ml) brown beef stock
4 tablespoons parsley
1 bayleaf
2 tablespoons (30 ml) tomato purée
1 tablespoon flour
½ oz (10 gm) butter
For the mashed potato:
1½ lb (675 gm) potatoes
¼ pint (150 ml) milk
1½ oz (35 gm) butter
salt and pepper

Peel, top and tail, and dice the carrots.

In a frying pan warm four tablespoons of oil. Peel, and finely chop the onion and the garlic cloves.

Add the onion and garlic to the frying pan. Fry gently. Whilst these are frying skin the tomatoes (see page 10) and chop finely. When the onions are brown add the tomatoes and continue cooking for 1½ minutes.

Add meat and diced carrots and fry for a further 8 minutes, stirring often. When the meat has completely turned brown add the stock until the meat is two-thirds covered, then season.

Add bay leaf, tomato purée and chopped parsley. Simmer for 1½ hours adding more stock

as needed. Stir occasionally during cooking. Peel, dice and cook the potatoes in boiling, salted water. Once tender, drain well and replace them in the saucepan over a low heat to dry out for a minute. Mash with a fork or potato masher.

Add the warmed milk and butter, beating well. Add seasoning and leave.

After the mince has been cooking for 1½ hours, mix 1 tablespoon of flour with the ½ oz (10 gm) butter and drop in small pieces into the mince. Stir to thicken and cook for a further 20 minutes. Put the meat in the bottom of a casserole dish, place the potatoes on top, smooth down and pattern with a fork. Bake for 25 minutes in an oven preheated to 375F/190C/gas mark 5, until brown.

Serve with fresh vegetables.

☆ ☆ ☆

Chef's tips:
☆ This dish may also be topped with grated cheese, to add to the flavour.
☆ Thickening of this dish must be done as in the recipe. If it is thickened at the beginning it will separate, leaving oil on the top.

POTATO AND SOUSED HERRING SALAD

Serves: 4
Type of dish: cold starter or lunch
Preparation time: 15 - 20 minutes
Waiting time: nil
Cooking time: nil
Suitable for dinner parties: no
Suitable for first course: yes
Special equipment: none required
Suitable for freezing: no
Calorie content: low
Carbohydrate content: average
Fibre content: low
Protein content: high
Fat content: low

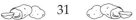

4 soused herrings (or rollmops)
3 medium-sized potatoes
1 large cooked beetroot
3 spring onions
2 fl oz (50 ml) French dressing
1 hard boiled egg, finely chopped
½ teaspoon dried dill or 2 teaspoons chopped fresh dill
salt and pepper
½ iceberg lettuce
½ Lollo Rosso lettuce

Chop the rollmops into dice. Slice the spring onions. Boil an egg and, when cold, chop it finely.

Peel, dice and cook the potatoes in boiling salted water, until tender.

When cooked, refresh the potatoes under cold running water for 5 - 10 minutes to prevent further cooking. Drain. Mix the rollmops, potatoes, spring onions, beetroot together in a bowl, add the dressing and toss well. Season.

Wash and break up the iceberg lettuce, placing the leaves in the base of the chosen serving dish.

Arrange the Lollo Rosso lettuce around the edges to add colour. Place the rollmop and potato mixture on top, then sprinkle with dill. Garnish with chopped egg. Around the edges place quartered tomato and a sprig of parsley to finish.

Chef's tips:

☆ When preparing lettuce never cut with a knife as this bruises the leaves and allows them to brown quickly. Always leave them whole until the last minute and then twist the leaves off.

☆ Do not prepare salad too far in advance.

POTATO AND CHEESE PIE

Serves: 4
Type of dish: hot main course or accompaniment to fish
Preparation time: 35 minutes
Waiting time: nil
Cooking time: 20 minutes
Suitable for dinner parties: yes as a vegetable
Suitable for first course: no
Suitable for microwave cooking: yes
Suitable for pressure cooking: no
Special equipment: casserole dish and frying pan
Suitable for freezing: yes
Calorie content: average
Carbohydrate content: low/average
Fibre content: low
Protein content: average
Fat content: low/average

1½ lb (675 gm) potatoes
2 medium onions
1 oz (25 gm) butter
salt and pepper
8 oz (225 gm) Cheddar cheese, grated
2 garlic cloves
1 teaspoon mixed herbs, finely chopped
½ teaspoon nutmeg
White sauce:
1½ oz (35 gm) butter
1½ oz (35 gm) flour
¾ pint (425 ml) milk

Peel the potatoes and place in cold, salted water. Make sure that all the potatoes are roughly the same size to allow even cooking.

Bring to the boil and simmer until the potatoes are cooked and then strain and allow to cool.

Meanwhile slice the onion finely, grate the cheese and peel and crush the garlic.

Fry the onion and garlic in the butter until they are soft but not brown.

Make a white sauce by melting the butter in a thick-bottomed saucepan. Remove from the heat and add the flour, mixing it in well to form a paste. Then gradually stir in the milk which should be slightly warmed to prevent lumpiness. Stir for five minutes over a low heat until the sauce thickens and then season with the salt and pepper.

Butter a medium-sized casserole or baking dish.

Slice the potatoes.

Preheat the oven to 350F / 180C / gas mark 4.

Make layers of potato, onion and cheese, lightly seasoning with salt and pepper between each layer.

Save a few potatoes for a layer at the top.

Cover the layered mixture with the white sauce and sprinkle with the herbs. Cover with the final layer of potatoes and dot with butter.

Cook in the preheated oven for 20 minutes until golden brown.

Chef's tips:
☆ Ideally served with a seasonal salad and freshly grilled fish with lemon butter.
☆ Suitable for vegetarians.
☆ When crushing the garlic, top and tail and peel. Use the flat side of a large knife to press down lightly on the clove. Use the palm of your hand. Once crushed, finely chop. This prevents the wastage that collects in a garlic press.

POTATOES & ROAST APPLE WITH SAUTEED LIVER

Serves: 4
Type of dish: hot main course
Preparation time: 1¼ - 1½ hours
Waiting time: 35 - 40 minutes
Cooking time: 5 - 8 minutes
Suitable for dinner parties: yes
Suitable for starter: no
Suitable for microwave cooking: no
Suitable for pressure cooking: no
Special equipment: ovenproof dish, large frying
   pan
Suitable for freezing: no
Calorie content: low
Carbohydrate content: average
Fibre content: low
Protein content: high
Fat content: low/average

2 lbs (1 kg) potatoes	
salt	
2 fl oz (50 ml) vegetable oil	
3 oz (75 gm) butter	
7 dessert apples	
four 7 oz (200 gm) slices liver	
ground black pepper	
1 tablespoon flour	
5 fl oz (150 ml) brown stock	
2 fl oz (50 ml) cider vinegar	
parsley to garnish	

Preheat the oven to 450F/230C/gas mark 8.

Peel the potatoes and turn into barrel shapes about 2 inches (5 cm) high, ¾ inch (2 cm) wide.

Put the potatoes in a pan of cold salted water and bring to the boil. Cook for 3 minutes then drain.

Mix the oil and butter together and keep to one side. Heat a little of the fat mixture in a large frying pan, add the drained potatoes and keep turning until well coated on all sides with the mixture.

Transfer to a roasting tray and roast for 20 - 25 minutes turning often until golden brown and tender.

Peel, core and cut the apples into quarters, then turn into the same shape as the potatoes. Heat another pan with a little of the oil mixture in. Add the apples, coat with oil then transfer to a ovenproof dish and roast for 15 minutes, until evenly coloured and tender. Remove and put to one side.

Trim the liver.

Heat a frying pan with the remainder of the oil and butter over a high heat, add the liver and brown for a couple of minutes on each side. Remove and put in a warm place together with the potatoes and apples.

Add a little flour to the fat remaining in the frying pan. Gradually mix in the stock and vinegar and cook for two minutes until thickened. Then season.

To serve, pour the thickened stock over the liver and garnish with alternating apples and potatoes, finishing with a sprig of parsley.

LANCASHIRE HOTPOT

Serves: 4 - 6
Type of dish: hot main course
Preparation time: 1¼ hours
Waiting time: nil
Cooking time: 2½ hours
Suitable for dinner parties: no
Suitable for first course: no
Suitable for microwave cooking: no
Suitable for pressure cooking: no
Special equipment: tall round pot or casserole
  dish
Suitable for freezing: no
Calorie content: average/high
Carbohydrate content: average
Fibre content: low
Protein content: high
Fat content: average

½ oz (10 gm) butter
8 medium potatoes, peeled and thickly sliced
salt and pepper
2 teaspoons dried thyme
2 - 3 lbs (1 - 1.35 kg) lamb chops
1 oz (25 gm) dripping (or butter)
3 medium onions, peeled and sliced
4 lambs kidneys, cored and sliced
4 oz (125 gm) mushrooms sliced
1 oz (25 gm) flour
1 pint (550 ml) well-seasoned brown stock
12 shelled oysters (optional)

Preheat oven to 325F/160C/gas mark 3.

Peel and thickly slice the potatoes. Peel and slice the onions, core and slice the kidneys and slice the mushrooms. Grease the inside of the chosen dish using half the butter.

Cover the base with half of the sliced potatoes, season with salt, pepper and thyme.

Brown the chops in some dripping in a heated frying pan. When brown lay them on top of the potatoes, and season.

Soften the onions in the dripping. Cover the chops with the onions, followed by the mushrooms, kidneys and oysters if you have them. Season again.

Finish with a layer of overlapping potatoes.

Warm the dripping that remains in the pan. Add the flour gradually, and stir in the stock. Strain onto the hotpot. Season again.

Dot the remaining butter around the top of the potatoes. Cook covered for 2 hours, then a further half hour uncovered, to brown.

☆　　☆　　☆

Chef's tip:
☆ Traditionally served with pickled cabbage.

HASH BROWN

Serves: 4
Type of dish: hot vegetable
Preparation time: 10 - 15 minutes
Waiting time: 30 minutes
Cooking time: 25 minutes
Suitable for dinner parties: no
Suitable for first course: no
Suitable for microwave cooking: no
Suitable for pressure cooking: no
Special equipment: grater
Suitable for freezing: no
Calorie content: low
Carbohydrate content: low
Fibre content: low
Fat content: low
Protein content: average

1 lb (450 gm) potatoes	
1 small onion	
salt and black pepper	
1 oz (25 gm) butter	
2 tablespoons vegetable or olive oil	

Peel and coarsely grate the potatoes and place in a colander. Remove as much moisture as possible by squeezing with your hands. Then leave to drain for 30 minutes.

Peel and finely chop the onion and mix with the potatoes. Add seasoning.

Heat the butter and oil in a frying pan on a medium heat.

Spoon the potato and onion mixture into the frying pan, packing it down well, leaving a small gap around the edges. Cook for 15 minutes over a gentle heat, until golden brown. Invert onto a plate, then gently slide back into the pan to cook the other side. Mark into four, using a sharp knife, and cook for a further 10 - 15 minutes.

Chef's tips:
☆ You can make four individual hash browns by dividing the mixture into four before cooking. Using a spatula or fish slice to shape and turn.

Make sure that it is packed down firmly in the frying pan, and do not be too anxious to

turn it (especially if making the larger one). It may result in the collapse of the dish.
☆ Ideally served with steak or chicken.

NIÇOISE SALAD

Serves: 6
Type of dish: cold starter or light lunch
Preparation time: 40 - 45 minutes including
   cooking potatoes
Waiting time: nil
Cooking time: potatoes only
Suitable for dinner parties: yes
Suitable for first course: yes
Special equipment: none
Suitable for freezing: no
Calorie content: low
Carbohydrate content: low
Fibre content: low
Protein content: low
Fat content: low

4 small new potatoes
4 oz (125 gm) green beans
3 hard boiled eggs
3 medium tomatoes skinned
½ green pepper, cut into julienne
½ red pepper, cut into julienne
½ iceberg lettuce
½ Lollo Rosso lettuce
8 oz (225 gm) canned tuna fish (drained)
10 canned anchovy fillets
1 red onion, thinly sliced
10 black olives

Vinaigrette:

3 tablespoons (45 ml) wine vinegar
salt and freshly-ground black pepper
3 tablespoons (45 ml) olive oil
6 tablespoons (90 ml) vegetable oil

Wash the potatoes, but do not peel.

Place in a saucepan covered in cold salted water. Bring to the boil, then reduce heat and simmer for 15 minutes, or until tender. Drain and refresh under cold running water. Once cooled, peel and slice into thin slices.

Top and tail the beans and cut in half crosswise. Cook for 10 minutes in boiling salted water. Cut eggs and tomatoes into quarters. Julienne the peppers. Slice the onion.

Prepare the vinaigrette by combining the vinegar and salt together, adding the oil, whisking well to blend. Season with the pepper.

To serve, combine potatoes, beans and green and red peppers in a bowl, toss in half the vinaigrette.

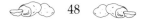

Arrange the iceberg lettuce in the base of a serving dish, with the Lollo Rosso neatly placed around the outside. Place the mixed vegetables in the centre. Flake tuna over the vegetables. Cut the anchovy fillets in half lengthways and arrange them on top of the tuna in a lattice design. Arrange onion rings around the base with the quartered tomatoes and hard boiled eggs, alternating for colour and presentation. Garnish with black olives. Then add the rest of the vinaigrette.

☆   ☆   ☆

49

Chef's tip:
☆ Add the vinaigrette only at the last minute before serving to retain the crispness of the lettuce.

POTATO BREAD

Serves: makes two ¾ lb (350 gm) loaves
Type of dish: light lunch served with honey or
   jam
Preparation time: 40 - 45 minutes
Waiting time: 2½ hours
Cooking time: 40 - 45 minutes
Suitable for dinner parties: as an accompaniment
Suitable for first course: no
Suitable for microwave cooking: no
Suitable for pressure cooking: no
Special equipment: two ¾ lb (350 gm) loaf tins
Suitable for freezing: yes
Calorie content: average
Carbohydrate content: high
Fibre content: average
Protein content: high
Fat content: average

½ oz (10 gm) fresh yeast or 1 tablespoon dried yeast
4 oz (125 gm) sugar
½ pint (275 ml) milk
6 oz (175 gm) butter
1 tablespoon salt
2 eggs, beaten
6 oz (175 gm) freshly-mashed potato
1½ lb (675 gm) white bread flour

Crumble fresh yeast, or shake dried yeast, into a large mixing bowl. Add l tablespoon sugar and 4 fl oz (125 ml) luke-warm water. Then stand for 10 minutes in a warm place.

Cut the butter into small dice. Warm the milk to blood heat and stir in the butter. Pour onto the yeast. Add the remaining sugar, beaten egg and salt, and mix well.

Boil and mash the potato and mix it in, beating with a wooden spoon until smooth. Add the flour gradually beating vigorously with a wooden spoon, stopping as soon as the dough clings together. Turn onto a floured surface and knead for 10 minutes, adding a little more flour if needed, until the dough is smooth.

Place in a lightly-greased bowl and cover with cling film, then leave in a warm place for 1¼ - 1½ hours, or until the dough has doubled. Heat the oven to 375F / 190C / gas mark 5. Punch down and knead the dough for a further five minutes. Divide into two and place in two buttered loaf tins. Place back in a warm area covered for a further 20 minutes, or until the dough has risen above the edge of the tins.

Bake for 40 - 45 minutes, or until the bread sounds hollow when gently tapped. Turn out and cool.

☆　　☆　　☆

Chef's tips:
☆ To make potato rolls, make in half quantities and divide dough after second kneading.

Bake for only 20 minutes. Makes 12 medium rolls.

☆ When proving, do not put dough in a place where it is likely to get too hot, as this will kill the yeast.

COBBLERS POT

Serves: 6
Type of dish: hot main course
Preparation time: 35 - 40 minutes
Waiting time: nil
Cooking time: 40 minutes
Suitable for dinner parties: no
Suitable for first course: no
Suitable for microwave cooking: no
Suitable for pressure cooking: no
Special equipment: ovenproof dish
Suitable for freezing: no
Calorie content: high
Carbohydrate content: average/high
Fibre content: low
Protein content: high
Fat content: average

4 oz (125 gm) back bacon
4 medium sized onions
2½ lb (1.15 kg) potatoes
2 soused herrings
12 oz (350 gm) sliced roast pork
2 tablespoons vegetable oil
1 teaspoon salt
1 teaspoon black pepper
½ pint (275 ml) milk
3 eggs, beaten
¼ pint (150 ml) soured cream
4 oz (125 gm) grated Cheddar cheese

Cut the rind off the bacon and cut the bacon into thin strips. Peel and thinly slice the onions. Peel and thinly slice the potatoes.

Gently heat a large frying pan with two tablespoons of oil. Add the bacon and the onions and fry for five minutes. Add the potatoes and fry until lightly browned.

Cut the herrings into strips. Cut the pork into small dice and mix with the herrings. Put a layer of potato mixture into a greased ovenproof dish. Spoon the mixed pork and herrings onto the potato mixture, then spread over the remaining potato. Smooth the top.

Mix together the milk, eggs and soured cream.

Pour into the ovenproof dish. Sprinkle with grated cheese and bake in a preheated oven (400F/200C/gas mark 6) for 40 minutes. Serve hot.

☆ ☆ ☆

Chef's tips:
☆ This recipe requires a large saucepan. An alternative method is to fry the potatoes in a separate pan in a little more oil and then mix with the bacon and onions.
☆ Serve with crisp vegetables or crusty bread.

GERMAN POTATO AND SMOKED BACON HOTPOT

Serves: 4
Type of dish: hot main course
Preparation time: 25 - 30 minutes
Waiting time: nil
Cooking time: 30 minutes
Suitable for dinner parties: no
Suitable for first course: no
Suitable for microwave cooking: yes
Suitable for pressure cooking: no
Special equipment: large frying pan
Suitable for freezing: yes
Calorie content: low
Carbohydrate content: average
Fibre content: low
Protein content: low/average
Fat content: low

1 lb (450 gm) smoked back bacon
1 lb (450 gm) potatoes
10 oz (275 gm) carrots
5 oz (150 gm) finely sliced leeks
3 tablespoons (45 ml) vegetable or olive oil
1 pint (550 ml) white stock (page 9)
2 teaspoons dried mixed herbs
1 bay leaf
½ teaspoon ground black pepper
1 large cooking apple
6 oz (175 gm) frozen runner beans
6 oz (175 gm) frozen broad beans
1 tablespoon cold water and 2 teaspoons cornflour (mixed to form a paste)

Trim the rind off the bacon and cut the bacon into strips.

Peel and dice the potatoes. Peel, top and tail, and slice the carrots at an angle.

Trim the white parts of the leeks and cut into thin slices. Discard the green parts.

Using a large frying pan or saucepan, fry the potatoes, bacon, carrots and leeks in the oil. When just beginning to colour, stir in the stock, herbs, bayleaf and pepper.

Bring to the boil and cover, simmering for 15 minutes. Peel, core and slice the apple. Stir it into the pan together with the frozen vegetables and cornflour mixture. Bring to the boil, stirring constantly.

Cover and cook for a further 15 - 20 minutes.

Remove bayleaf and serve garnished with a sprig of parsley, together with a fresh, crusty roll.

☆   ☆   ☆

Chef's tip:
☆ When you have peeled and sliced the apple, place it in a bowl of cold water with a little lemon juice to prevent it from going brown before it is needed.

POTATO SOUFFLÉ

Serves: 6
Type of dish: hot accompaniment to meal
Preparation time: 35 - 40 minutes
Waiting time: 20 minutes.
Cooking time: 30 - 35 minutes.
Suitable for dinner parties: yes
Suitable for first course: no
Suitable for microwave cooking: no
Suitable for pressure cooking: no
Special equipment: 2 pint soufflé dish
Suitable for freezing: no
Calorie content: average/high
Carbohydrate content: high
Fibre content: average
Protein content: high
Fat content: average

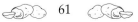

3 tablespoons fresh white breadcrumbs
1 tablespoon almonds, finely-chopped
1 lb (450 gm) potatoes
3 eggs
2 extra egg whites
3 fl oz (75 ml) double cream
1½ oz (35 gm) grated Parmesan cheese
salt and pepper
pinch each of paprika and nutmeg
2 tablespoons chopped chives

Butter a soufflé dish that can hold two pints, then coat with the breadcrumbs and finely-chopped almonds.

Remove any excess by tipping out. If you are unable to get the almonds to stick, sprinkle them onto the base lightly. Place in a fridge and chill for 30 minutes.

Preheat the oven to 375F/190C/gas mark 5. Remove all the shelves except the central one, and place on it a baking tray which is large enough to hold the soufflé dish. Make sure that it is sturdy and will not bend with the application of heat.

Peel the potatoes and simmer in salted water for 20 minutes. Once the potatoes have cooked, drain them well, using a colander. Then purée them by placing them through a sieve, and leave to cool.

Separate the eggs. Then add the two extra whites to the other whites in a large mixing bowl.

Beat the yolks with a large spoon, then mix in with the cream and grated cheese. Add this to the warm potato purée, mixing well. Then sea-

son.

When the oven has reached the required temperature add a pinch of salt to the egg whites. Whisk the whites vigorously until they are stiff and start to peak when the whisk is pulled up.

Put two tablespoons of the whipped egg white into the potato purée and stir them in.

Add the potato to the egg white and fold in gently using a plastic spatula or slotted spoon. Do not beat. Stir in the rest of the ingredients gently.

Pour into the chilled soufflé dish and place in the preheated oven upon the baking tray. Cook for 30 - 35 minutes until well risen and golden brown on top.

Chef's tip:
☆ Serve immediately. Do not keep opening the oven when the soufflé is cooking because this will prevent the soufflé from rising.

FISH CAKES

Makes: approximately 25 fish cakes
Type of dish: hot main course
Preparation time: 1 hour including boiling of
   potatoes
Waiting time: 20 - 25 minutes (boiling potatoes)
Cooking time: 6 minutes (fried), 20 - 30 minutes
   (baked from frozen)
Suitable for dinner parties: no
Suitable for first course: no
Suitable for microwave cooking: no
Suitable for pressure cooking: potatoes only
Special equipment: potato masher, fish slice,
   heavy-bottomed frying pan
Suitable for freezing: yes
Calorie content: average
Carbohydrate content: average/high
Fibre content: average
Protein content: high
Fat content: average

3 lbs (1.35 kg) old potatoes	
1 lb (450 gm) can pilchards in tomato	
bunch of parsley	
flour for dusting	
dot of butter per fish cake, if baking	

This is a dish which is pre-eminently for the freezer. It is the ideal way of using up a large volume of floury old potatoes at the tail end of the season and going into the mass-production business. Choose a day when you might like fish cakes for supper. You can then keep enough of them aside, while freezing the majority.

If you have the luxury of fresh parsley in your garden, you will need handfuls of it.

The recipe is immensely simple and consists of only three basic ingredients, potato, cans of pilchards, and parsley. You can make as many or as few as you wish. Just make sure that your freezer has enough room to hold trays of the fish cakes, each fish cake separated from the other.

Peel and boil the potatoes in salted water until tender. Remove from the heat, drain thoroughly, and immediately mash well. Place the mash into a large bowl. Allow the potato to cool for about 10 minutes.

While the potatoes are cooling remove the pilchards from the cans, retaining the fluid. Remove and discard the bones. Then break the pilchards up while mixing them with your hands into the mashed potato, incorporating at the same time the fluid.

Wash and shake dry the parsley. Take a handful, assembled so that all the stalks are towards

you. Lightly squeeze the leaf ends so that they are relatively compact and, holding the parsley over the mixture, snip off the top end, one eighth of an inch (2 - 3 mm) at a time. Mix in the parsley with your hands.

Flour a surface. Remove a well-rounded tablespoon of the mixture (about 2 ounces (50 gm)), round it in your hands to the shape and size of the fish cake required (make them this small as they are very rich) and turn them in the flour, coating them well.

Dust some baking sheets with flour. Arrange the fish cakes on them so that they do not touch each other. Set aside enough for the evening meal and place the remainder in the freezer. When frozen, take them off the trays and place them in suitable storage containers with lids, and re-

place in the freezer.

To cook the unfrozen fish cakes, redust with flour. Heat vegetable oil in a frying pan until it just starts to smoke. The amount of oil will depend upon the number of fish cakes being fried but as a general guide it should be about one eighth of an inch (2 - 3 mm) deep. Cook on a high heat until the underside is golden and brittle, about 2 - 3 minutes. Turn over and repeat the process for the second side.

The frozen fish cakes should be defrosted before frying and generously dusted with flour before cooking. Cook as above.

The still frozen fish cakes may alternatively be baked in a hot oven (425F/220C/gas mark 7) with a dot of butter on top for approximately 25 minutes, turning after 10 minutes and redotting with butter.

Chef's tips:
☆ These fish cakes tend to hold quite a lot of moisture. Baking in the oven enables some of the moisture in them to evaporate while cooking.
☆ The amount of pilchards can be adjusted to taste.
☆ Other highly-flavoured fish may be used as an alternative to pilchards, such as tuna.

BAKED POTATO STUFFED WITH POACHED EGG

Serves: 4
Type of dish: light lunch
Preparation time: 1 hour - 1¼ hours
Waiting time: 5 minutes whilst browning.
Cooking time: 35 - 40 minutes
Suitable for dinner parties: no
Suitable for first course: yes
Suitable for microwave cooking: yes
Suitable for pressure cooking: no
Special equipment: none required
Suitable for freezing: no
Calorie content: average
Carbohydrate content: average
Fibre content: low
Protein content: high
Fat content: low

4 medium-sized potatoes	
4 poached eggs	
¼ pint (150 ml) Mornay sauce	
3 oz (75 gm) cooked ham	
3 shallots or 1 small onion	
1 oz (25 gm) butter	
1 tablespoon oil	
¼ teaspoon ground nutmeg	
salt and pepper	
4 tablespoons double cream	
fresh breadcrumbs	
grated Parmesan	

Use four evenly-sized potatoes. Prick lightly with a fork and bake in a oven preheated to 400F/200C/gas mark 6 for 1 hour or until soft.

While the potatoes are cooking, lightly poach 4 eggs. If you do not have a pan specifically designed for poaching, use a saucepan or deep-sided frying pan, containing just enough simmering water to cover the eggs. Add a pinch of salt and a little vinegar.

When the eggs are cooked, remove, using a slotted spoon and drain well.

Make ¼ pint (150 ml) of Mornay sauce as shown on page 10.

When the potatoes are cooked and soft to touch remove from the oven and cut a cross in the top of each with a sharp knife. Then open them out by squeezing gently at the base of each. Leave to cool slightly.

Slice the ham into strips. Peel and slice the shallots thinly.

In a frying pan, with half the butter and cooking oil, lightly fry the shallots until they are transparent, but do not colour.

Scoop out two-thirds of the potato carefully with a teaspoon. Mix the removed potato with the nutmeg, butter, salt and pepper and beat well.

Divide the shallots between the four potatoes laying them in the hollow of each.

Place one tablespoon of Mornay sauce into each, covering the shallots. Top with the sliced ham, the potato mixture and one tablespoon of cream in each. Then put the poached egg gently

on top, covering the ham. Cover with another tablespoon of Mornay sauce and finally sprinkle with breadcrumbs and grated Parmesan cheese.

Bake in the oven until golden brown on top.

☆ ☆ ☆

Chef's tip:
☆ Serve with a salad garnish and a sprig of parsley.

INDIAN CURRIED POTATOES WITH YOGHURT

Serves: 6
Type of dish: hot lunch or light evening meal
Preparation time: 35 - 40 minutes
Waiting time: nil
Cooking time: 20 - 25 minutes
Suitable for dinner parties: no
Suitable for first course: no
Suitable for microwave cooking: no
Suitable for pressure cooking: no
Special equipment: electric liquidizer
Suitable for freezing: no
Calorie content: low / average
Carbohydrate content: average
Fibre content: average
Protein content: high
Fat Content: low

1 large onion
3 garlic cloves
1 small chili pepper
2 large tomatoes
8 medium-sized potatoes
oil for deep frying plus 7 tablespoons oil
½ teaspoon stem ginger
½ teaspoon coriander
½ teaspoon cumin
2 bay leaves
½ oz (15 gm) butter
½ teaspoon ground nutmeg
1 tablespoon flour
1 tablespoon tomato purée
1 teaspoon curry paste
½ pint (275 ml) brown stock
1 tablespoon mango chutney
salt and pepper
5 tablespoons natural yoghurt
2 tablespoons chopped parsley

Peel and finely chop the onion and garlic.

Remove seeds from chili pepper and chop the flesh. Concasse the tomatoes, (cover them in boiling water, stand for 10 - 20 seconds, drain and peel skin off, remove seeds and then chop roughly).

Peel the potatoes and cut them into thin chips.

Combine the onion and garlic in a liquidizer and process until puréed.

Heat 2 inch (5 cm) of oil in a saucepan, add potatoes and cook over a high heat until they are golden brown, but still firm. Drain on ab-

sorbent paper.

Place the 7 tablespoons of oil in a frying pan or saucepan and gently fry the onion and garlic purée, chili and stem ginger. When light brown add the coriander, cumin, bayleaf, butter and nutmeg, stirring well.

Add the flour to soak up any excess fat. Add the tomato purée and the curry paste and stir well in.

Gradually add the stock. Stir in the mango chutney, salt and pepper and tomatoes. Add the potatoes and cook over a medium heat, occasion-

ally stirring lightly.

Cook covered for a further 20 - 25 minutes until potatoes are tender and well-coated in the reduced sauce.

To avoid breaking the potatoes up, do not stir too harshly.

Add the yoghurt and mix well. Serve hot, topped with chopped parsley.

☆   ☆   ☆

Chef's tips:
☆ This is a very mild curry. If a hotter dish is desired just add a little more curry paste or curry powder.
☆ If cooking for vegetarians replace brown stock with water or vegetable stock.
☆ Wash chopping board well after working with onions and make sure the onions are not near you, especially if they make you cry. As with chopping chilies, you should never let them contact your face or eyes.

POTATO, COURGETTE AND AUBERGINE MOUSSAKA

Serves: 4
Type of dish: hot main course
Preparation time: 1¾ - 2 hours
Waiting time: nil
Cooking time: 25 - 30 minutes
Suitable for dinner parties: yes
Suitable for first course: no
Suitable for microwave cooking: no
Suitable for pressure cooking: no
Special equipment: casserole dish or baking tray
Suitable for freezing: yes, but best eaten fresh
Calorie content: average/high
Carbohydrate content: average/high
Fibre content: low/average
Protein content: high
Fat content: average

1 aubergine	
3 courgettes	
1 lb (450 gm) potatoes	
2 tablespoons oregano fresh, or 1 tablespoon dried	
salt and black pepper	
3 tablespoons olive oil	
4 tablespoons breadcrumbs	
4 oz (125 gm) grated Cheddar cheese	

For the tomato and garlic sauce:

1 medium-sized onion
2 garlic cloves
4 oz (125 gm) red split lentils
1 oz (25 gm) butter
1 oz (25 gm) flour
14 oz (400 gm) can chopped tomatoes
1 tablespoon tomato purée
1 pint (550 ml) vegetable stock
¼ pint (150 ml) dry white wine

White sauce:

2 oz (50 gm) butter
2 oz (50 gm) flour
1 pint (550 ml) milk
3 oz (75 gm) grated Parmesan cheese
3 eggs
salt and pepper

Preheat the oven to 400F/200C/gas mark 6.

Top, tail and thinly slice the aubergine.* Top, tail and thinly slice the courgettes. Peel the potatoes and slice them as thinly as possible.

In a casserole dish or baking tray, layer the

aubergine, potato and courgette, seasoning with salt, pepper and oregano, and pouring 1 tablespoon of olive oil between each layer.

Cover with lightly greased foil and bake in the oven for 25 minutes.

Meanwhile, you can make the sauces, beginning with the *tomato and garlic sauce.*

Peel and dice the onion and peel and crush the garlic. Rinse the lentils well under cold running water and leave to drain in a colander.

Lightly fry the onion and garlic in a frying pan with 1 oz (25 gm) butter, do not colour. Cook until the onion is soft and transparent. Add the flour and stir in well. Remove from the heat, add the tomatoes and tomato purée.

Gradually add the vegetable stock and wine, stirring. Add the lentils and bring to the boil stirring often. Simmer for 5 minutes, then leave to one side.

Check the aubergines etc in the oven.

Start to make the *white sauce.* Put the milk into a saucepan and bring to the boil.

Melt the butter in a saucepan over a medium heat. Add the flour and mix well. Gradually add the boiled milk, stirring continuously.

Bring to the boil and simmer for 15 minutes until the sauce begins to thicken. Stir in the Parmesan, salt and pepper. Whisk in the eggs and cook for a further 5 minutes, then turn off.

Pour the tomato and garlic sauce over the aubergines etc.

Cover the top with the white sauce.

Sprinkle with the breadcrumbs and grated Cheddar cheese.

Cook for 30 minutes at 400F / 200C / gas mark

6. Then reduce oven to 375F/190C/gas mark 5 and cook for a further 5 minutes.

Remove from the oven once the top has turned golden brown and the cheese has completely melted.

Serve with fresh vegetables or just crusty bread.

Chef's tips:

☆ * To make the aubergines softer and less bitter place them in a colander after slicing. Sprinkle with a tablespoon of salt and leave to drain for 15 minutes. Rinse them under cold running water and then pat dry with paper towels.

☆ Garnish with a sprig of fresh parsley.

☆ This dish is ideal for vegetarians.

STUFFED POTATO BALLS

Serves: 4 - 6
Type of dish: hot first course
Suitable for first course: yes
Preparation time: 45 - 50 minutes
Waiting time: nil
Cooking time: 15 - 20 minutes
Suitable for dinner parties: yes
Suitable for microwave cooking: no
Suitable for pressure cooking: no
Special equipment: potato masher, frying pan.
Suitable for freezing: no
Calorie content: average
Carbohydrate content: average
Fibre content: low
Protein content: high
Fat content: average

3 lb (1.35 kg) large potatoes
¼ teaspoon salt
¼ teaspoon black pepper
pinch each of ground nutmeg, coriander and paprika
1 egg, beaten
Stuffing:
6 shallots finely-sliced or 1 small onion
3 garlic cloves
2 tomatoes
1 oz (25 gm) butter
8 oz (225 gm) minced beef or lamb
1 teaspoon chopped parsley
½ teaspoon chopped mint
For frying:
olive or vegetable oil.
2 eggs
salt and pepper

Peel the potatoes and place in a saucepan covered with cold salted water.

Bring to the boil and simmer until tender and well cooked. Drain, then mash.

When cool, add the salt, pepper, nutmeg, coriander and paprika. Then beat in the egg.

Now make the *stuffing*. Finely slice the shallots and peel and crush the garlic. Skin the tomatoes as shown on page 10.

Melt the butter in a frying pan on a medium heat and add the shallots and minced meat. Fry until brown, then add the garlic and tomato, parsley and mint. Then season.

Cook until the meat is cooked, then drain and

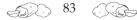

leave to cool.

Take out one tablespoon of the potato mixture and place it on a floured surface. Make into a circle using your hands, to around 2 inches (5 cm) in diameter. Make sure that it is not too thick, around ¼ inch (1.25 cm) is ideal.

In the centre of the potato place one teaspoon of the meat. Then wrap the potato around to form a ball. Roll in the palm of your hand until smooth. Continue with this technique until all the potato and meat mixture has been used.

For *frying,* heat a frying pan on a medium heat with oil covering the base.

Beat the eggs and add the salt and pepper.

Dip the balls three at a time into the egg mixture, then fry until golden brown on all sides. Remove, drain and keep warm in a low oven, until they have all been cooked.

Chef's tip:
☆ Serve hot on a green salad. You may also serve this dish with a variety of dips.

In the same series:

Others in preparation